Children's Room

in a weekend

Children's Rooms

in a weekend

Roo Ryde

BETTERWAY BOOKS

CINCINNATI, OHIO

Acknowledgments

I dedicate this book to Mr Shoes, Pishi, Lobi, my sister and best friend Lisa, Mum, and Dad for their
loving support and patience with this project and for allowing me to clutter up their houses with
all my bits and pieces; Dominic Blackmore for his brilliant photography, calm approach to everything,
and great lunches!; Anna Ryder-Richardson of Squidgy Things for her expert sewing skills and ability
to keep laughing whatever time of day; Adrian and Albert for always being on hand to help me out;
and Sara Colledge at Merehurst Fairfax, who never failed to come up with a solution to the problems
I encountered. Also a big thank you to everybody else who was involved with this project and helped
me to create the colorful results.

Please note that the projects in this book have been
designed for the rooms of children, not for those of
babies or young toddlers.

Distributed to the trade and craft markets in North America in 2002 by
Betterway Books
an imprint of F&W Publications, Inc.
4700 East Galbraith Road
Cincinnati, OH 45236
(800) 289-0963

ISBN 1-55870-618-6

A catalog record for this book is available from the Library of Congress.

Editor: Geraldine Christy
Designer: Anthony Cohen
Photographer: Dominic Blackmore
Stylist: Roo Ryde
Artwork: Brihton Illustration

Color separation by Dot Gradations, England
Printed in Singapore by Tien Wah Press

Contents

Introduction

Although I am a firm believer in trying to create rooms for children that will grow with them, I also love to include as much color, texture, and as many elements of fun as possible. I have found that one can combine both these ideas and still produce a practical bedroom that can also stimulate thought and imagination in a child's mind.

Most parents start off with the best of intentions when their first child comes along, and they take great pleasure in planning and decorating the baby's room. But as your first child grows up and maybe another one or two babies arrive, in between trying to juggle a job and organize the whole family you might suddenly realize that

your child's room does not offer the sort of stimuli and excitement that is needed.

Bear in mind that a well-planned room with plenty of storage space and a work station will not only make life easier for your child but also for you. If your children are happy with their rooms they will be more content to play and do their homework in them and, perhaps, more willing to keep them neat!

So let your creativity run wild and involve your children in the decisions and choices for their rooms—remember that at the end of the day you can close the door on it all while they are left alone to enjoy their own private fantasy land.

Great decorating ideas do not need to depend on spending a lot of money or on having beautifully proportioned rooms—in fact, few of us have the means to live in the style that we all dream about. I have tried to be cost-conscious when planning all the projects in this book and often they include items that you may already have lying around the house. If not, they can easily be picked up on a low budget or by second hand.

I hope that you will enjoy making the projects that I have created for this book. Practical, easy-to-follow steps are provided for all of them and you need no special skills—just a weekend! But do bear in mind that the projects are not designed for you to follow slavishly. If you prefer to adapt or interpret my designs to give different

effects then go ahead. Try to incorporate your children's favorite colors, favorite stories or cartoon characters, their sports and hobbies. Most of the projects are suitable for both boys and girls, but some of them may have a more feminine or masculine appeal. I hope that you can draw inspiration even from those that are not immediately appropriate for your children.

Since I have no formal training I think of myself as a "layperson's designer." Many of the techniques that I have used for the projects are designed to save time and are based on experience. More often than not I try to combine steps, but if you feel more comfortable breaking some of the steps down into additional stages, feel free to do so. The important point is to achieve a satisfactory end result.

I have tried to keep the instructions as clear and as uncomplicated as possible. Any points that need further explanation can be found in the tinted advice boxes that accompany the detailed steps to the projects.

You will notice that in many of the photographs that accompany the steps I have used mainly white cotton thread for sewing. This has been done so that it shows up well in the demonstrations—but when you machine or hand sew fabric, do try to use a matching colored cotton thread so that it is less visible.

I have tried to make all the projects as colorful and eye-catching as possible. But besides looking great they all have a practical element to them—they are all well worth spending a weekend on. You may find some of the projects will take up most of your time over a weekend, while others can be completed more quickly.

So go ahead and surprise your children with one of these wonderful weekend projects. I guarantee you that not only will they be grateful, but also you will be very proud of the end results.

Good luck.

Button cornice and holdbacks

A bright button theme provides a splash of color that will enliven any window. Children love to choose the colors, so enlist their help to make the buttons.

Windows come in all sorts of shapes and sizes, and deciding how to dress them without spoiling their shape always challenges my imagination. An easy and effective solution is to create an illusion. Dress a small window grandly and it suddenly takes on a new look. Hang curtains so that they cover part of a window that is disproportionately large for the room and the window seems smaller.

Irregularly shaped windows, especially in children's rooms, can be used to your advantage and transformed into eye-catching features. There are no hard and fast rules to adhere to. Kids love bright and bold rooms, so get them actively involved in deciding on the look.

The window that we have worked around here is an average-sized sash window. Creating the cornice and holdbacks for it, with their button theme, brings in an element of fun. Once you have made the cornice and holdback bases you could turn them into whatever else you like—such as a flower theme, funny faces, or if your child is crazy about auto racing, for instance, steering wheels for the holdbacks and racing cars along the cornice.

Planning your time

DAY ONE

AM: Cut or buy particle board and prime all the wood pieces

PM: Paint pieces in chosen color

DAY TWO

AM: Paint design on holdbacks and make clay buttons

PM: Finish painting design and assemble project

Tools and materials

Two particle board disks, ⅝" (1.5cm) thick, 12" (30cm) in diameter

Two particle board backplates, ⅝" (1.5cm) thick, 6" (15cm) square

Two pieces of wooden dowel, 1" (2.5cm) in diameter, 8" (20cm) long

One shaped length of cornice and brackets

Primer paint

Gloss paint in two colors

Two paintbrushes

One pair of brightly colored shoelaces

Polymer clay in a selection of colors

All-purpose glue

Drill and drill bits

Selection of screws and plastic anchors

Awl

Masking tape

All-purpose spackle

Heavy brown paper for templates (if cutting your own shapes out of particle board)

Day One

Step 1

Prepare all the wood pieces. Each holdback requires a backplate, a wooden dowel, and a front button plate. These need to be pre-drilled before priming. The backplates need a screw hole in each corner and one in the center. The dowel needs a screw hole in each end and the button needs a screw hole right in the center. The four other holes on the button, for the laces, need to be drilled with an extra-large drill bit.

Step 2

Using primer, paint all the pieces of wood to seal the surface. Then allow them to dry. When the wood is dry, using your chosen paint color, paint all the pieces of wood and again allow to dry. Try to apply the paint with even strokes for a smooth color finish.

Step 3

Screw the dowel into the backplate with a 1½" (4cm) long screw inserted from the base of the backplate.

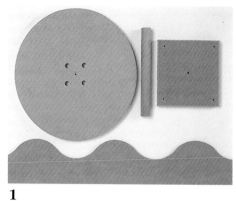

1

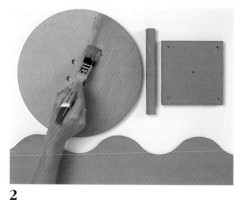

2

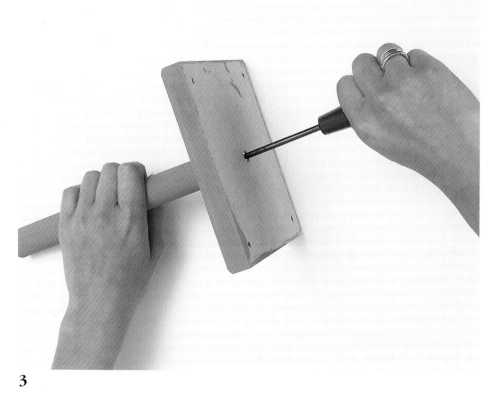

3

Cutting the pieces

If you have a jigsaw, you may prefer to cut the particle board pieces yourself. Otherwise, I recommend that you get your local hardware store to do it for you.

If you decide to use a jigsaw, draw a template for each shaped piece (button and cornice) on heavy brown paper. The button backplate can be measured and drawn directly on the piece of particle board. Place the paper template on the particle board, and using a pencil, trace around the outlines onto the wood.

Following the pencil lines, cut out the particle board shapes with the jigsaw. Use a workbench for sawing so that you can secure the piece to be cut in a vise.

Day Two

Step 4

Using masking tape, mask off the first stage of the design on the button front. Measure and divide the face into five sections and mask them off, leaving ⅜" (1cm) in between to paint. Using a contrasting paint color, paint the lines and allow to dry. If you rest the button on top of a paint can, it will make it a lot easier to work on.

Step 5

When the first set of lines are completely dry, repeat Step 4, this time masking off the lines in the opposite direction. Paint and allow to dry.

Step 6

Using an awl through the screw holes, mark the wall exactly where you want the holdbacks to be positioned. Drill these four holes and place a plastic anchor that matches the screw size into each hole. Then screw the backplate onto the wall.

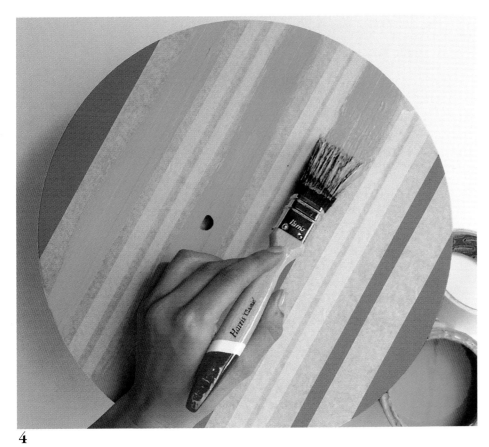

4

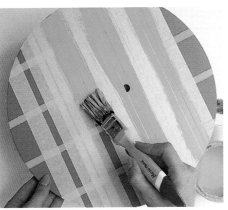

5

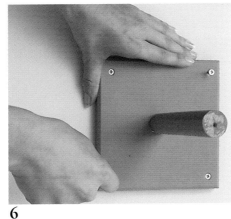

6

Painting wood

Although I might not always explain in detail in the steps, it is important that you prime all never-before-painted surfaces. Beware of "all-purpose" primer paints—buy one that is specifically designed for the type of surface on which you are working.

For all the projects in the book, a white primer combined with an undercoat is the quickest option. For the top coat, unless otherwise instructed, choose an oil-based paint; it will leave you with a more durable surface.

Step 7

With the button front positioned centrally over the wooden dowel, place a screw into the center hole and screw the two pieces together. Use a small amount of spackle to cover the head of the screw and disguise it. Then paint over it, and when it is dry, thread the laces through the four holes.

Step 8

Once the completed holdback is in position, drape the curtains behind it.

Step 9

Using a selection of different colors of polymer clay, roll out sausage shapes and cut these into fat disks. Gently roll these with a small rolling pin to flatten them. Create different designs by adding other colored pieces or try rolling two colors together for a marbled effect. Make either two or four holes in each button, using a long, pointed implement. Place the clay buttons on a baking sheet and bake for the manufacturer's specified time, and then allow them to cool.

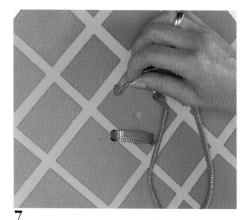

7

8

9

Using polymer clay

Polymer clay is an easy material to work with and is available in a large range of colors from craft stores and children's toy shops. It is a "clean and dry" clay—you will not end up with a mess everywhere—and it is ideal for children to play with. Follow the manufacturer's instructions on the package when baking the clay. Baking it hardens the clay and makes it very durable.

Step 10

Lay the piece of cornice down and position the buttons until you are happy with the effect. Then, working from one end, glue them in place. Allow them to set before moving the cornice.

Step 11

The cornice should be attached to two brackets placed over the window for a really secure attachment. (See *Putting up the cornice board*.) This decorative treatment will transform the plainest window or dullest room into something quite spectacular.

Putting up
the cornice board

Determine the location for the cornice by aligning it with the window or ceiling. If they are not parallel, use a level as a guide. Using the brackets, mark the drilling points through the bracket attachment holes with a pencil. Drill the holes and push plastic anchors into them. Screw in the brackets, and attach the cornice to the brackets.

10

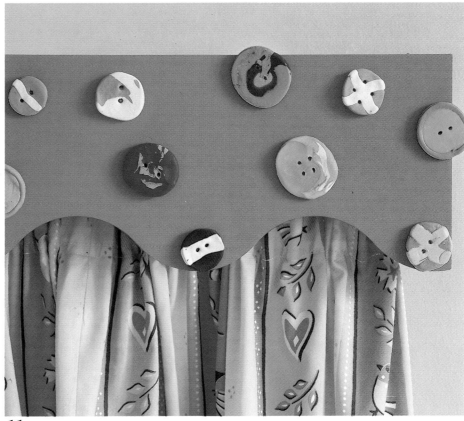

11

Bow canopy and bedding

A feminine and simple solution for a dull bedroom that will delight young ladies of all ages. This elegant bow theme has been followed through to create matching bedding.

Children seem to grow up much faster nowadays and from an early age they know exactly what they want—from the style of clothes they wear and toys they choose to the design of their rooms. But for girls who just want to be girls, it is fast and easy to give their bedrooms a face-lift with a few feminine touches.

This elegant bed canopy operates on a very simple principle. Once the rail has been attached to the wall you simply clip the fabric to the rings hanging from it. I bought about 11yds (10m) of cheap cheesecloth and hemmed it at the top and bottom. With selvages on each side of the cheesecloth, I did not need to sew side seams. But what made the canopy look extra special were the jumbo stuffed bows that I used to tie back the cheesecloth.

If you want to take the bow theme one step further you could cut out some strips of material from a coordinating fabric, hem them, and then tie them into bows through the metal rings on the bed canopy rail. You could also add a matching fabric border all the way down the inside edges of the cheesecloth canopy. I followed the bow theme through to the comforter cover and pillowcases. Both of these are easy to make and both use the same method.

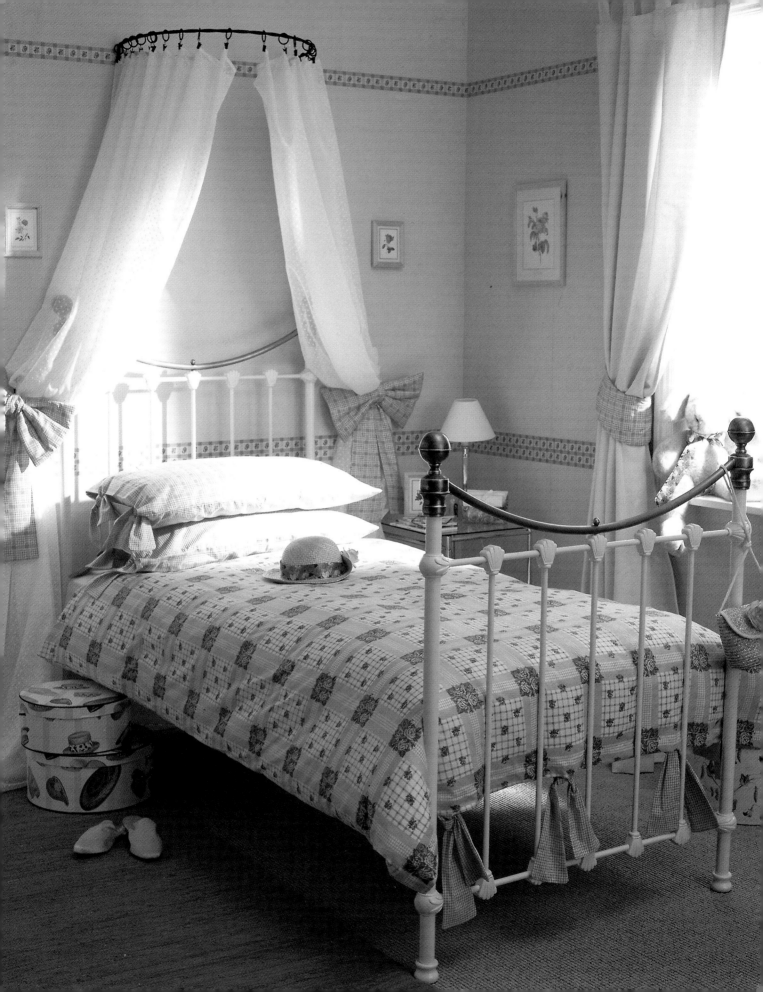

1

Day One

Step 1

For each canopy bow you will need to cut out: two pieces of fabric 10x16" (25x40cm) and one piece of batting the same size for the body of the bow; one piece of fabric 5x7" (12x18cm) for the center loop; two fabric shapes following pattern A on page 70 (cut these on the double with the fold of the fabric along the 3½" (9cm) side so that you have long, narrow pieces for the bow tails); one piece of ribbon 10" (25cm) long.

Step 2

Place the bow body pieces right sides together, with the piece of batting beneath them both. Machine sew this "sandwich" all around the edge, leaving an opening about 5" (12cm) wide on one of the long sides. Push the pieces through the opening to turn the material right side out, so that the batting is now sandwiched in the middle (see page 55). Hand sew the opening.

Step 3

Place the two bow tail pieces made from pattern A right sides together. Machine sew all the way around, leaving an opening on one of the long sides. Turn right side out and hand sew the opening. Iron flat.

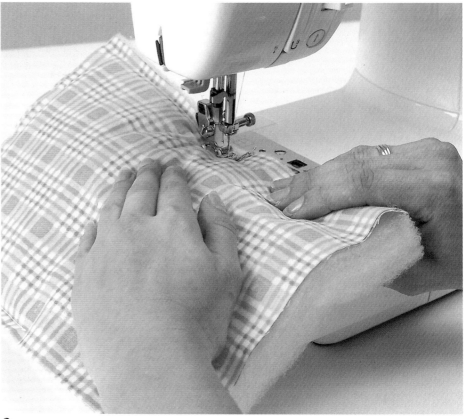

2

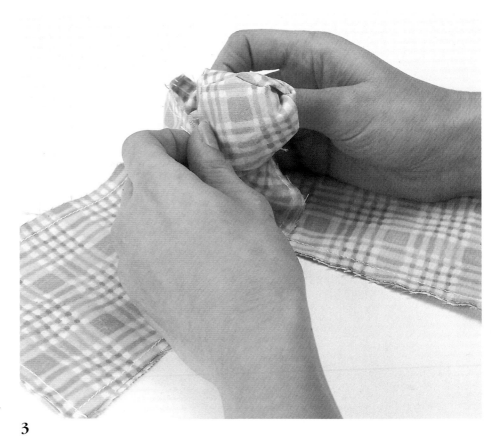

3

Step 4

Using a hot iron, press a ¾" (2cm) hem along each long side of the center loop. Wrap the loop around the center of the stuffed bow body to form the bow shape, and hand sew the loop ends together.

Step 5

Feed the long bow tails through the center loop that you have just sewn, so that the tails are of equal length. Then feed the ribbon through the loop in the same way. It is this ribbon that will secure the bow to the holdback hook.

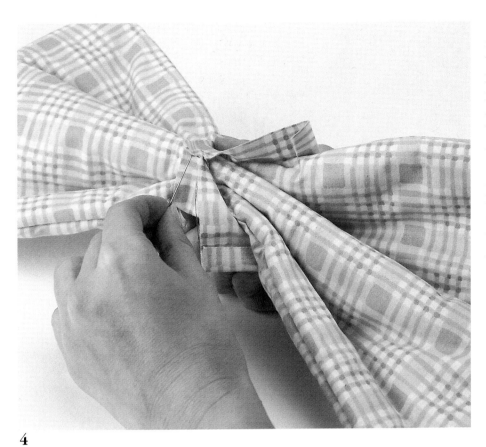

4

5

Making the comforter cover and pillowcases

The comforter cover and pillowcases are both made in the same way, although the steps describe how to make the pillowcase. Remember, however, when making the comforter cover, that it has three ties along the bottom, not two as for the pillowcase. To make the cover you can use either an extra-wide sheeting fabric or other easy-care material. For a twin cover the fabric must be 58" (145cm) wide.

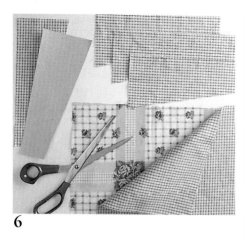

6

Day Two

Step 6

For each pillowcase cut two pieces of contrasting fabric 22x30" (55x75cm) and four fabric shapes following pattern B on page 70 (cut these on the double with the fold of the fabric along the 2" [5cm] side). For the comforter cover similarly cut two pieces of contrasting fabric 58x84" (145x210cm) and six fabric shapes following pattern B.

Step 7

Pair all the tie pieces, right sides together, and machine sew around them, leaving a small opening through which you can turn them right side out. Then press them flat.

Step 8

With wrong side facing up, press in ⅜" (1cm) of fabric along the top and bottom edges of the pillowcase opening. Fold over another 1½" (4cm) of fabric, press, and then machine sew along the edge. Position both the ties on the folded hem for the pillowcase (but note there will be three ties for the comforter cover) and machine sew in place, one row of stitches at the base of the tail and one higher up near the edge.

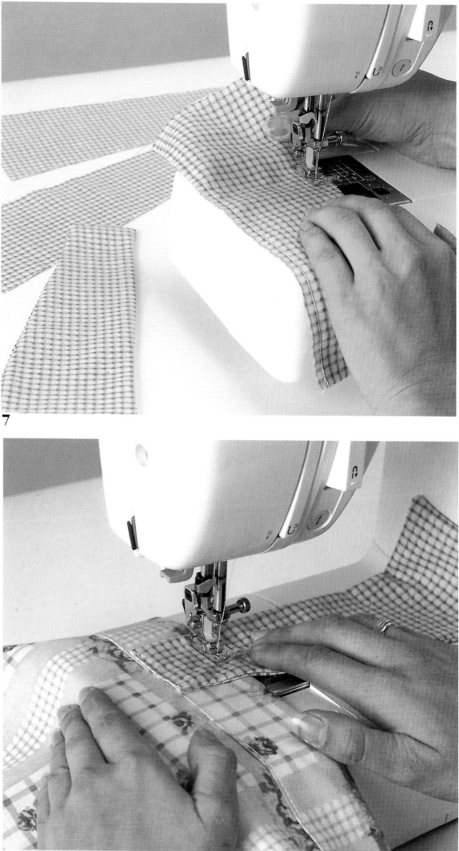

7

8

9

Step 9

To assemble the pillowcase, sew French seams on the remaining three sides. To do this, place the wrong sides of the fabric together, machine sew around the three closed sides, then turn the pillowcase inside out, right sides together. Make sure that you have pulled out all the corners, then press flat along the seam lines. Next, sew a second seam ⅜" (1cm) from the first (which is now the folded edge). Turn right side out and press the seam allowance flat to one side of the seam.

Step 10

Screw a tieback hook into the wall on both sides of the bed, making sure that there is a good 6" (15cm) clearance from the bed edge. Using the ribbon on the back of the bow, tie it around the cheesecloth drapes, pull them back, and secure to the hook.

10

Pom-pom chair and cushion

Cheer up an old chair with a multitude of colors and a bright, comfortable cushion. Then, for a smart and fun look, paint other furniture in the room to match.

Most people have a plain wooden chair in their house somewhere. This project shows you how such an ordinary piece of furniture can be transformed into a unique and colorful child's chair that is sure to be treasured.

Look beyond the framework of the chair and see the possibilities for creativity. The simple wooden chair featured here looked completely different once it had been painted, and once some fun wooden balls had been screwed into the top of the chair frame. Continuing the theme, I designed a cushion for the chair decorated with colorful balls and trimmed with coordinating pom-pom fringe.

The theme then extended to a small, round occasional table, which was given a new lease on life using the same paint colors and decorated with the ball design. Even the curtain in the room ties in with the scheme, with the addition of its pom-pom fringe.

Be adventurous with your choice of colors, but do make a test run first to make sure that they all fit comfortably together. Once you are happy with your color combinations you will find all sorts of pieces that you can paint.

Planning your time

DAY ONE
AM: Sand chair and wash it down; paint one color

PM: Paint other colors

DAY TWO
AM: Cut out cushion and design

PM: Sew cushion

Tools and materials

Plain wooden chair

Fine-grit sandpaper

All-in-one white primer and undercoat

Satin-finish colored paints

Paintbrushes

Fabric for cushion base

Pillow form

Fabric for design on cushion

Pom-pom fringe (or other trim)

Scissors

Masking tape

Two round wooden door knobs (optional if the chair is for a young child)

Two double-ended screws

Day One

Step 1

Choose three or four paint colors for the chair and cushion trim to match them. Two wooden door knobs complete the chair.

Step 2

Using fine-grit sandpaper, gently rub down the chair all over to provide a good key, or rough surface, for your primer and paint. If you are going to add wooden balls, drill holes in the top of the frame and in the knobs. When you have finished sanding, use a damp cloth to wipe the chair down.

Step 3

After priming the chair, decide which colors to paint different parts of the chair and use masking tape to mask any adjoining edges while you paint each color. Paint the two wooden door knobs.

1

2

3

Priming the chair

Although it is not shown in the steps, it is important that you prime all never-before-painted surfaces (see page 11). For the wooden chair, I used an all-in-one white primer and undercoat. For the top coat, I chose a satin-finish oil-based paint, as this gives a more durable surface.

Day Two

Step 4

When the chair and knobs are dry screw the knobs into place on each side of the chair frame using a double-ended screw. The chair can be varnished to protect the paint finish. I recommend that you varnish any item that is going to be placed in a child's bedroom so that it can withstand wear and tear. General-purpose oil-based varnishes and polyurethane varnish are the toughest wearing and most waterproof.

Step 5

Cut out two pieces of fabric 17x17" (42x42cm) for the cushion cover and two circles 3" (8cm) in diameter for each circle to be sewn on. You will also need 64" (160cm) of your chosen trim.

Step 6

Place the fabric circles right sides together and machine sew them all the way around. Make a small slit in the center on one side, clip around all the edges, and then turn the circle right side out. Lightly press with an iron.

4

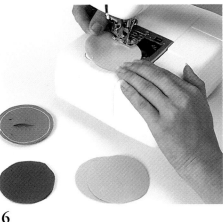

5

6

Attaching the knobs with double-ended screws

Wooden door knobs are available in a variety of shapes, and adding them to the chair gives a special touch. If they are not pre-drilled, it will be necessary to drill a hole into them and a corresponding one into the chair where you want to attach them. Connect them with a double-ended screw. This looks similar to a screw with no head and must be the same size as the holes you drill.

Step 7

Pin on all the circles in the desired positions on the top piece of the cushion. Then machine sew them all around their edges.

Step 8

Working on the right side of the top piece of the cushion, machine sew the pom-pom fringe all the way around.

Step 9

Place the bottom piece of the cushion with the top piece, right sides together. Machine sew around three sides and halfway down the fourth one, making sure to sew right on the edge of the pom-pom fringe tape.

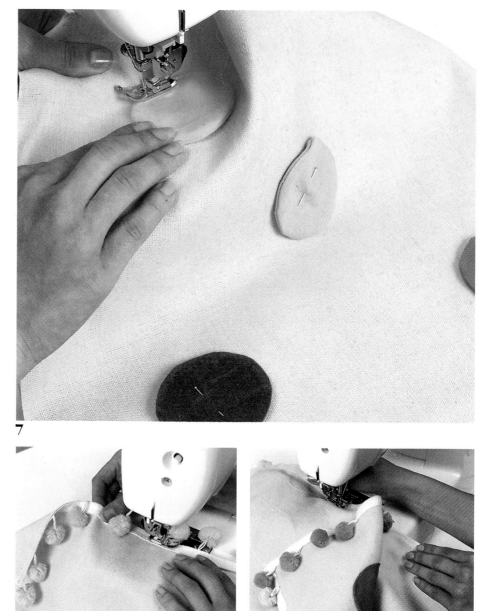

7

8

9

Choosing trims

If you cannot match up the colors for your trim, look for inexpensive ones and dye them yourself. The pom-pom fringe that I used was dyed using cold water dyes to match the colors of the fabric appliqué shapes. Cold-water dyeing is quick and easy to do. Simply dissolve the dye and dye fixative in the stated amount of water, following the manufacturer's recommended guidelines, and then submerge the trim. Check every 10 minutes until the trim has the depth of color that you require. Remove, rinse, and hang to dry.

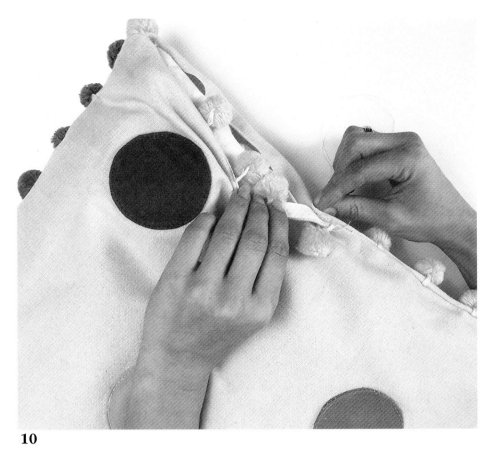

10

Step 10
Turn the cushion cover right side out and put the pillow form inside. Hand sew the opening.

Step 11
Once you have mastered the methods involved in making this cushion, why not try designing your own, using different shapes and fabrics, or make a reversible cushion that has an interesting detail on both sides.

11

Hand sewing openings

Use a slipstitch when openings or seams must be sewn by hand from the right side of the fabric. To do this, take the needle across the opening and make a small stitch ⅛" (2mm) long along one side of the opening, then take the needle across the opening and make a similar stitch on the other side, closing the two sides together. Continue to the end and then tie the thread off in the seam.

Fat-cat beanbag

Floor seating is always popular with children and this cat will soon become a well-loved friend. Adapt the idea to make other animal beanbags.

Not only lovable but also practical, this cuddly fat cat is comfortable to sit on. Its body and head are filled with pellet-sized styrofoam balls, which are available from fabric stores or the craft departments of major stores. Like many of the projects in this book, the fat cat is very easy to adapt to other shapes and sizes. Whatever animal beanbag your children want or whatever colors coordinate best with their rooms, as long as you follow the same basic steps, you can cut out and make a whole host of different animals.

For the base of the animal's body, choose a fairly dark color and make sure that it is a heavyweight, durable fabric; this part will receive the most wear and tear. For the additions that turned the bag into a cat I used both felt and cotton twill.

You may wish to make the outer cover removable and washable. To do this, cut out a second head and body shape, about 1¼" (3cm) smaller all the way around. Use this as an inner lining, machine sewing it all the way around and leaving a hole to put the styrofoam balls into. Then fill this inner shape with the balls and hand sew to close the opening. This body shape can then be stuffed inside the "real" animal, and the base of the outer animal secured with Velcro or snaps.

Planning your time

DAY ONE
AM: Cut out all the pieces

PM: Machine sew the face together

DAY TWO
AM: Machine sew the paws together

PM: Assemble the cat

Tools and materials

Black heavy-duty fabric

Two contrasting fabrics

2oz (55g) batting for the tail (you can also add batting to the face and paws)

Pellet-sized styrofoam balls

Pinking shears

Scissors

Thick brown paper for templates

2

3

1

4

Day One

Step 1

Enlarge the templates on page 71 to the size you require and trace around them on brown paper to make your own templates. The body of the cat I made measured 48" (118cm) from head to base and 30" (75cm) across the width. Use the enlarged templates to cut out all the pieces, using pinking shears for the body pieces. Cut two pieces for the body, head, and ears from one piece of black fabric; one black base circle with a diameter the same as the body base (in this case 30" [75cm]); two black tail pieces and one piece of batting for the tail; two white felt cheeks; two pink noses; two pink tongues; four white eye bases; four black eyes; four white felt paws; and 12 pink paw pads.

Step 2

Pair all the pieces (excluding the body) with right sides together. Machine sew around the edge of each pair, make a slit in the center on one side (with the exception of the tongue and tail) and turn right side out. For the tongue, leave the top straight edge open to turn

right side out. For the tail, place the batting under the fabric and machine sew around the edge, leaving the base part (straightedge) of the tail open. Use a long tool to help you poke the tail through. (See page 55 for a more detailed explanation on machining and turning through.)

Step 3

Pin the pink nose onto the center of the white cheeks and machine sew it

all the way around. Then machine sew the whisker details using black thread.

Step 4

Machine sew the right-side-out black eyes onto the right-side-out white eye bases and then position the eyes on the front body piece and sew in place. Next, position the cheek piece with the top of the tongue inserted underneath, then machine sew this in place all the way around to secure it.

Day Two

Step 5

Position the pink paw pads on the white paws and machine sew in place.

Step 6

Position both paws on the front piece of the cat body and machine sew all around to secure in place.

Step 7

Place the two cat body pieces right sides together and insert the stuffed tail between the two layers at the base of the body where you want its final position to be. Machine sew all around the body except along the base. Repeat this row of stitches again for extra strength.

Step 8

With the cat still inside out, pin the base circle in place and machine sew it all around, leaving an opening to turn the cat right side out. Repeat this row of stitches again for extra strength.

Step 9

Fill the cat's body with the styrofoam balls and hand sew the opening closed. When pouring the styrofoam balls into the cat's body, ask someone to help you because these little balls have a static charge and tend to jump everywhere.

5

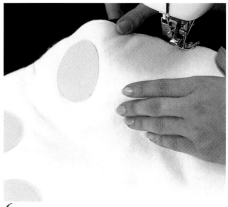

6

7

8

9

Machine sewing

A plain seam sewn with a straight stitch is the simplest and most versatile means of joining two pieces of fabric together. If you are not used to sewing with a machine, always pin the pieces of fabric together before sewing.

Sports rack and equipment bag

A handy rack will help children keep their sports equipment together and easy to find. They will enjoy transporting it all in a specially designed equipment bag.

Sweaty uniforms left festering in a bag under the bed are not the most pleasant of treats to come across—especially when they have been there for a while! So what better way to encourage your children to hang up their uniforms and equipment than their very own themed rack and wipeable sports bag? At least then you will have a reasonable idea of where to find the offending items!

The rack is very easy to make and can be topped with any sort of ball, from tennis to soccer, and from hockey to football—whichever is your child's favorite sport. I have used soccer balls here.

The bag is made from cotton-backed PVC, which means that it has the added benefit of being wipeable whenever necessary. Instead of putting your child's initials on the bag you could put their full name or nickname, date of birth, favorite team, or favorite player's name and number. Make sure you use a heavy-duty needle on your sewing machine when sewing the PVC. Make a practice run on fabric scraps because you will find PVC slightly different to work with than other fabrics.

Planning your time

DAY ONE
AM: Prepare rack; prime and paint it

PM: Make clay soccer ball disks

DAY TWO
AM: Cut out the paper templates and bag pieces; glue on numbers and letters

PM: Machine sew bag components together

Tools and materials

For the rack:
¾" (2cm) thick particle board, measuring 5x26" (13x65cm)

Five wooden dowels, 3" (7cm) long, ⅜" (1cm) in diameter

Drill

Primer paint

Gloss paint

Permanent marker

Wood glue

White polymer clay

For the equipment bag:
Cotton-backed PVC—one color for the bag, and two colors for the trims

64" (160cm) of brightly colored rope

All-purpose glue

Thick brown paper for templates

1

2

3

Day One

Step 1

For the rack, mark five evenly spaced points on the piece of particle board. Using the drill with a head piece the same size as the dowels, drill five holes into the base, stopping before you go all the way through the wood. Apply primer to the rack base and wooden dowels, and when the primer dries, paint them with the gloss paint, for a tough durable finish. When the paint is dry, place a little spot of wood glue into each hole along the rack base and insert the dowels.

Step 2

Using the white polymer clay, roll out five disk shapes, each ⅜" (1cm) thick, and make an indentation into the back of each one the same size as the dowels. Bake according to the manufacturer's instructions. When cool, use the permanent marker to draw on the soccer ball design (see template on page 72). You may want to do this in pencil first. Place a little spot of wood glue into the indentation on the back of each disk and glue onto the end of each dowel on the rack base.

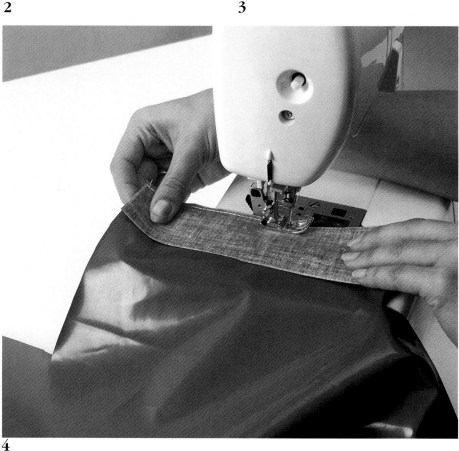

4

Day Two

Step 3

Following the pattern on page 72, cut out a template for the T-shirt bag from brown paper and then cut out the PVC. You will need two blue T-shirt base pieces excluding the red trim edges marked by dotted lines; four pieces of red sleeve borders, 2x8" (5x20cm); two pieces of red bottom trim 2x30" (5x74cm); one white circle 12" (30cm) in diameter, initials, number, and periods in whichever contrast color you prefer.

Step 4

Place the red sleeve and base trims right sides facing down on the dotted line edges of the blue T-shirt and machine sew along the edge. Do this for both the front and back pieces of the T-shirt.

Step 5

Using the all-purpose glue, stick the number onto the white circle. When this has dried stick the circle onto the front piece of the T-shirt. Glue the initials and periods under the circle.

Step 6

Place the right sides of the T-shirt together and machine sew down side A from top to bottom (see pattern on page 72).

Step 7

Open out the two sides flat with the wrong sides still facing you and fold over the top 2" (5cm) of side B all the way across the two T-shirt pieces and machine sew. This makes the rope channel.

Step 8

Fold the two sides back so that the T-shirt is right sides together again. Starting in a direct line from under the channel opening, machine sew along sides C and D.

Step 9

Turn the bag right side out and feed the rope into the channel. You may find it easier to do this if you attach a safety pin to one end of the rope. You can then feed the safety pin through the channel a little at a time and use it to pull the rope along (the pin will slide through the channel more smoothly than the rope and is easier to grip onto through the fabric). Take the rope ends and tie them together into a large knot.

Where to buy rope

I bought my rope from a boating shop. Marine supply stores sell colored ropes of varying thicknesses that are usually used for hoisting up sails!

5

6

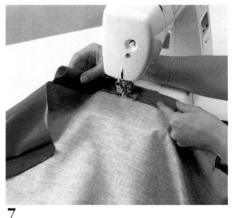

7

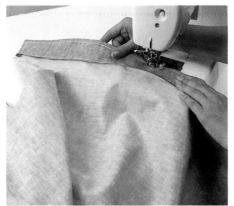

8

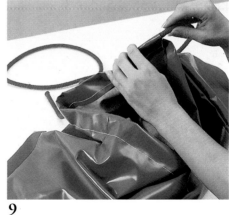

9

Fabric-fronted shelf units

These attractive storage units provide an opportunity for "everything in its place." They are easy to make and the decoration can be matched to any color scheme.

Teaching children to be organized and neat requires a lot of patience—they sometimes think that closets and drawers are for filling to excess and when it comes to retrieving a particular item can pull absolutely everything out until they find what they are after. It is possible, though, to make putting away and finding things less frustrating for them, by providing enough practical storage space. Open shelving is ideal because everything is immediately visible—but of course that does not guarantee that each shelf will be kept tidy!

For this project, I took a plain, free-standing wooden shelf unit, painted it a bright color, then added some fun shelf trim to the edge of each shelf and made a PVC cotton-backed fabric panel for the front. The cover simply rolls up and down and is held in place with plastic-coated hooks.

This idea can be translated to any size of shelf unit, and if you wanted, you could add a fabric panel to both the sides. Since these side panels would be permanently rolled down you would not need to put hooks into the sides.

Planning your time

DAY ONE
AM: Prime and paint shelf unit, trims, and wooden dowel

PM: Glue on edge trims; stick on Velcro

DAY TWO
AM: Make fabric cover panel

PM: Make clay fittings and screw in hooks

Tools and materials

Wooden shelf unit

Pre-cut particle board edge trim

Wood primer

Eggshell or gloss paint in two colors

Paintbrushes

Wood glue

Masking tape

Velcro

Cotton-backed PVC fabric (width and height of the shelf unit plus an extra 3" [8cm] all around)

Wooden dowel, ⅝" (1.5cm) in diameter, 2½" (6cm) wider than the unit

Colored polymer clay

Six plastic-coated screw-in hooks

Awl

Small tacks

Hammer

Day One

Step 1

Apply primer to all the bare wood. Then, using the two different color paints, paint the frame of the shelf unit in one color and the shelves and edge trims in the other color. Allow to dry.

Step 2

Apply wood glue to the front edge of each shelf and attach the edge trim in place. Use masking tape to secure it in place until the glue has completely dried.

Step 3

Take one side of the Velcro tape, cut it to the width of the top shelf, and then stick it on.

Day Two

Step 4

Cut the cotton-backed PVC to just under the total width of the unit—this is so that some of the brightly painted verticals will show on both sides of the cover. Hem the top by turning it over 2" (5cm) and machine sewing it.

Step 5

Take the other side of the piece of Velcro, stick it over the top hem of the fabric panel, and machine sew it in place for added strength.

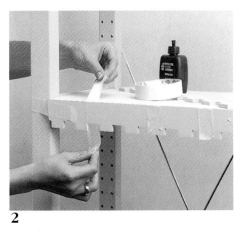

1

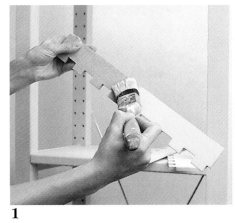

2

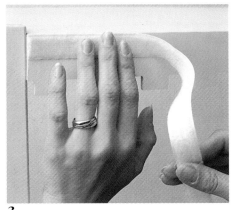

3

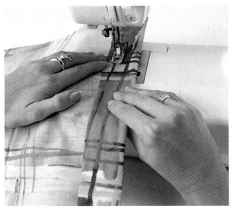

4

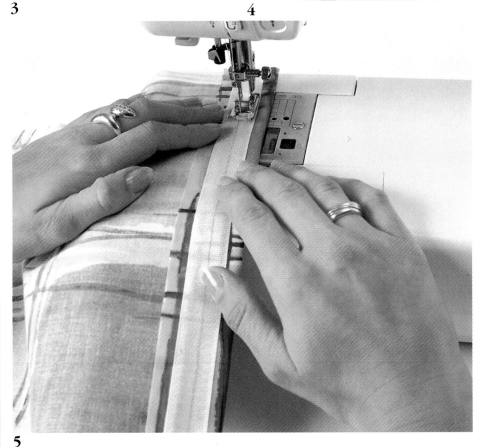

5

Painting the unit

Use an oil-based paint to paint the shelf unit since this will result in a more durable finish. Make sure that you paint the unit in the direction of its wood grain. Thus, apply paint to the vertical struts in up and down strokes, and paint the shelves from side to side.

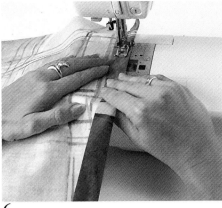

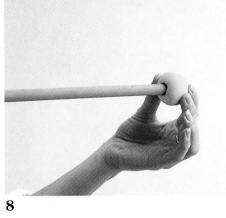

6

7

8

Step 6

Working on the bottom of the fabric panel, turn over ⅜" (1cm) and machine sew a hem. Then turn over another 2" (5cm) and machine sew this on the edge so that it forms an open channel—this is where the wooden dowel will be fed through. (PVC cotton does not fray, so you do not need to hem the side edges.)

Step 7

Apply primer to the wooden dowel and allow to dry. Then paint the wooden dowel with your chosen color, and when it is dry, feed it into the bottom channel of the fabric panel. Make sure that it protrudes an equal amount on each side. Then, using small tacks, tack from the back of the panel to secure the dowel in place—make sure the tack is hammered right through the fabric and into the dowel.

Step 8

Using the polymer clay, roll a round ball for each end of the dowel, one in each color. Before baking the balls, use the dowel to make an indentation into each of them to be sure that they will fit neatly onto it. Bake the balls following the manufacturer's instructions. When they are cool, apply a small amount of wood glue on the end of each piece of wooden dowel, and then stick the clay ball in place.

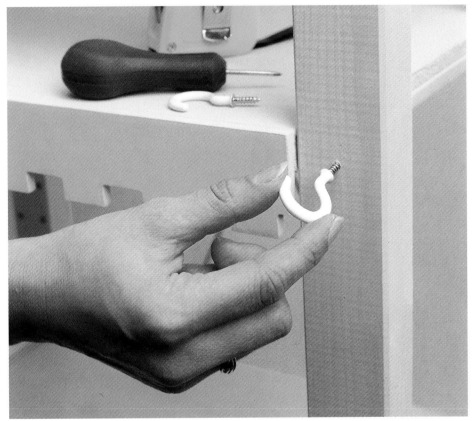

9

Step 9

Using a pencil, mark where the hooks are going to be positioned. Ideally, the first pair should be a quarter of the way down the vertical struts, the second pair halfway down the struts, and the third pair three-quarters of the way down. Then use the awl to make the holes, and screw the hooks in place. Finally, stick the fabric panel onto the Velcro strip at the top.

"Daisy daisy" bulletin board

An easy-to-change bulletin board is ideal for children to display an endless array of drawings, photographs, and messages, without marking the walls of their rooms.

Children love to personalize their rooms, but their belongings often end up all over the place. This is quite natural, but with careful thought and planning for their storage and shelving requirements you can help to encourage your children to be a little neater.

This fun bulletin board is ideal for holding pictures, cards, and any small items that are likely to be lost. You can make it as large or as small as you want and, of course, change the number of ribbons that crisscross it so that more items can be held in place or displayed.

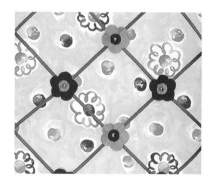

You can also choose your own theme for the fabric cutout shapes that cover and secure where the ribbons cross and continue whatever theme is in the design of the fabric. Or you could cut out the letters in your child's name and use these to cover where the ribbons cross.

For a more durable finish, I recommend that the piece of fabric that you use to cover the bulletin board be given a stainproof treatment first. This means that any dirty finger marks can be easily washed off.

Planning your time

DAY ONE
Prepare all your materials and staple the fabric to the board

DAY TWO
Attach ribbons and shapes

Tools and materials

A piece of particle board, 24x36" (60x90cm)

4oz (115g) batting, measuring 24x36" (60x90cm)

Fabric to fit the size of your board plus 3" (8cm) extra all around

⅜" (1cm) wide satin ribbon in two colors

Decorative tacks or pushpins

Felt in two colors

Pinking shears

Scissors

Staple gun

Hammer

Day One

Step 1

Cut the batting to the same size as the piece of particle board. Place the board on top of the fabric, allow 3" (8cm) all the way around, and cut with pinking shears.

Step 2

Place the fabric wrong side up and place the batting on top, then place the board on top of the batting.

Step 3

Pull the fabric tight, and along the middle of each side, place a few staples.

Step 4

Fold each corner over neatly and secure with staples, making sure that the fabric is pulled very tight.

Day Two

Step 5

Turn the board over so that the right side faces out. Lay strips of ribbon in one color from side to side diagonally across the board. Cut the strips, leaving an extra 3" (8cm) at each end.

Stainproof treatment

Fabric can be given a staining or waterproofing treatment, and it is possible to do this at home using kits available from department and fabric stores. This treatment will give your board the added benefit of being wipeable.

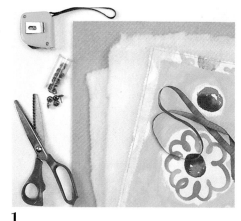

1

2

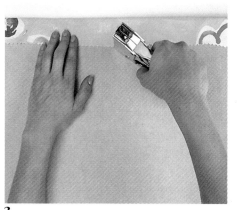

3

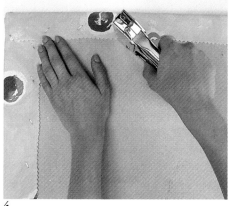

4

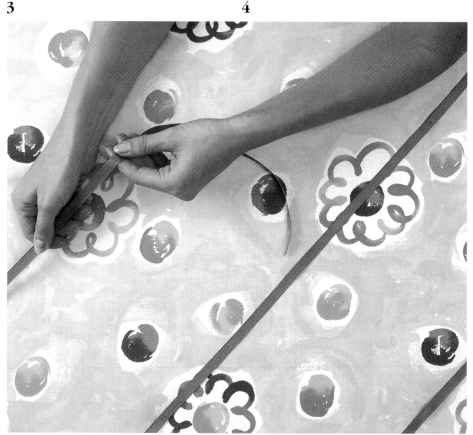

5

6

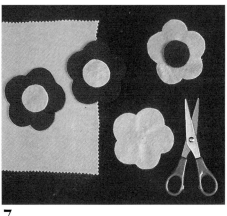
7

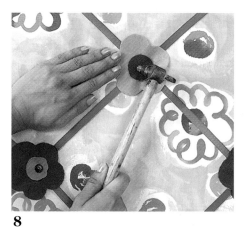
8

Step 6
Now lay strips of ribbon in the other color in the opposite direction. Again cut the ribbon strips, leaving an extra 3" (8cm) at each end.

Step 7
Cut out the daisy shapes and center piece from felt in alternating colors, following the template on page 70.

Step 8
Place a daisy and its center over each point where the ribbons cross and secure in place with a decorative tack or pushpin.

Step 9
Turn the board over and secure all the ribbon ends in place using a staple gun, making sure to pull them very tight. Finally, fasten two picture hooks into the back of the board for hanging.

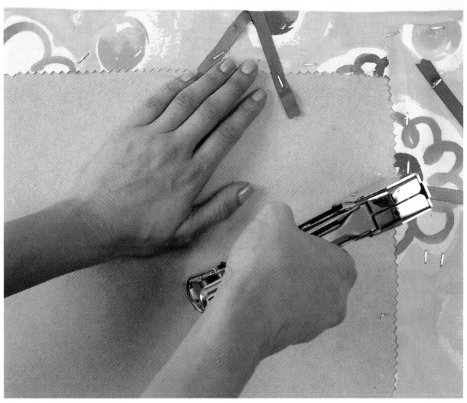
9

Tacking the fabric
If you do not have a staple gun you can use small tacks and a hammer, but you may need help in keeping the fabric tight.

Tic-tac-toe headboard game

This giant tic-tac-toe headboard game is positioned so that your children can enjoy a last challenge or two before settling down to sleep for the night.

Getting children to bed is not the easiest of tasks, especially when they have friends sleep over and it is practically impossible to get them to settle down. That is why the logic behind this headboard game is ideal, because they can play with it while in bed.

The board is made from felt and the playing pieces simply attach to it with Velcro. The whole game then hangs from loops on a piece of wooden dowel supported by two wall hooks.

This project can be adapted to make other board games. If you like a challenge you could try chess, checkers, or "Chutes and Ladders." For a large-scale game, however, it might be more practical to make a board that can be used on the floor. These games are ideal to take when traveling, because they can be folded up and packed in a bag.

Planning your time

DAY ONE
AM: Cut out all the pieces

PM: Make the board

DAY TWO
AM: Make the playing pieces; paint the dowel

PM: Make the clay shapes

Tools and materials

Felt in four different colors for the board, dividing lines, and playing pieces

2oz (55g) batting for the playing pieces

4oz (115g) batting for the board

A wooden dowel, 37" (92cm) long

Wood glue

Primer paint

Eggshell or gloss paint

Polymer clay in two colors to match the playing pieces

Heavy brown paper

Scissors

Velcro

Day One

Step 1

Cut out three pieces of blue felt for the hanging loops, each measuring 7x16" (18x40cm); two felt pieces and one piece of batting for the board, each measuring 36x36" (90x90cm); and four white felt pieces for the dividing lines, each measuring 2x36" (5x90cm).

Step 2

Mark on one piece of the blue felt board where the white lines should be positioned so that they divide the board evenly into nine squares. Machine sew them in place along each long side.

Step 3

Fold the felt loops in half lengthwise, right sides together. Machine sew along the long side and then turn it right side out. You do not need to sew the two ends. Position the three loops pointing downward at the top edge of the board on the right side and machine sew the ends onto the edge.

Step 4

Place the two blue board pieces right sides together, then place the batting underneath them. Machine sew all the way around, leaving about 8" (20cm) open along the bottom. Pull the board through the opening and then hand sew it closed.

1

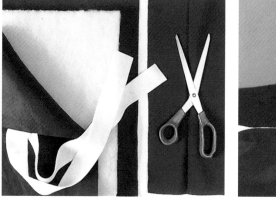

2

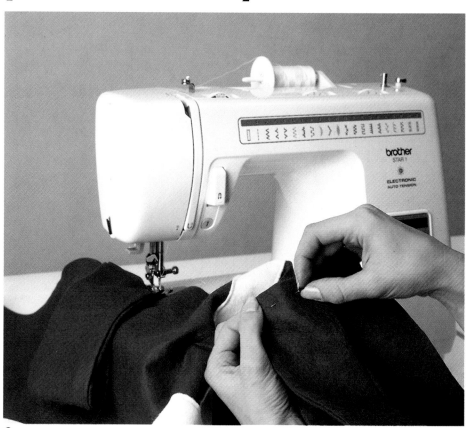

3

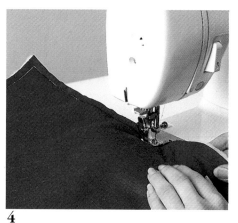

4

Choosing felt

Felt comes in different qualities and it is worth buying a heavyweight felt for the game board, but use a lighter weight one for the playing pieces.

Day Two

Step 5

Trace the outlines on page 70 and enlarge to make templates for the Xs and Os out of brown paper, remembering to allow a little extra all the way around for seam allowance. Cut out five pairs of each shape and a piece of batting for each pair.

Step 6

Place each pair of Xs and Os right sides together, and place the batting underneath. For each X, machine sew all the way around, leaving a small opening. Pull the X through this opening and then hand sew it closed. For each O, machine sew all the way around, then make a slit on the back through one layer of fabric and pull the O through the slit to turn it right side out.

Step 7

Attach two pieces of Velcro to the back of each O and X, and then sew up the slit on the back of each O.

Step 8

Paint the dowel with primer and allow to dry. Then paint with a satin-finish or gloss-finish paint and allow to dry.

Step 9

Make an X and an O shape out of polymer clay. For the X, roll out two long sausage shapes, then cut one in half and stick the two halves onto the other piece. For the O, roll out a ball, then gently roll it flat and make an indentation in it. Bake the shapes following the manufacturer's instructions. Stick them onto the wooden dowel using a touch of wood glue. Feed this through the felt loops and the board is ready for hanging. (Be sure that you make the Xs and Os the right size to fit through the board's loops.)

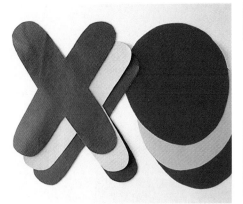

5

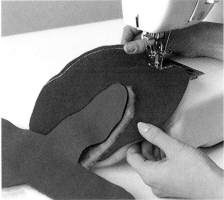

6

7

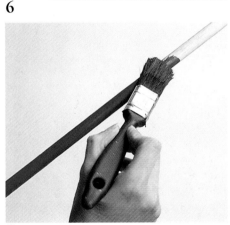

8

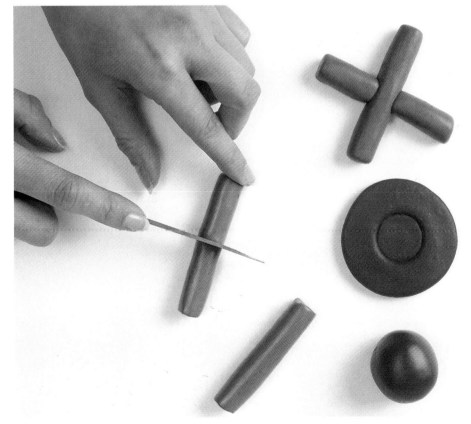

9

Eight-drawer chest

A little time and planning—and multicolored splashes of paint—transform an ordinary chest of drawers into an exciting and unusual piece of furniture.

I have always firmly believed that it is not worth spending a fortune on children's furniture, not only because it receives poor treatment but also because it is all too quickly outgrown. Fortunately, stores nowadays are full of self-assembly and plain wooden furniture that is ideal for applying a nice finish to.

The plain eight-drawer chest that I used for this project started off its life as a very basic unit, but with the addition of some fun color, tissue paper, and unusual handles it has assumed a new identity. For simplicity you could just pick out two colors of paint for drawers and create a dramatic checkerboard effect—especially if painted in black and white.

Look for really eye-catching handles or buy plain wooden ones and paint them to match the unit. You could also make interesting shapes out of polymer clay and glue them onto the fronts of the wooden handles. Feet added to the unit give it elegance, and painted appropriately, it would even be worthy of being kept in an adult's room.

Planning your time

DAY ONE
AM: Sand, drill, and color wash the unit and drawers

PM: Color wash the feet and glue them on; cut and attach paper shapes

DAY TWO
AM: Varnish the unit and drawers twice

PM: Varnish the unit a third time and attach the handles

Tools and materials

One plain eight-drawer chest

Sandpaper

Drill

Different colors of water-based paint

Paintbrushes

Plastic cups

Four wooden door handles (for the feet)

Wood glue

Different colors of thick tissue paper

Scissors

Artist's spray glue

Clear matte varnish

Eight decorative handles

Screwdriver

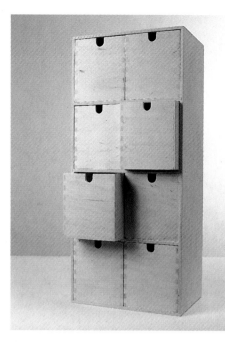

1

Day One

Step 1
Take each drawer out of the unit. The backs of the drawers will become the fronts (the existing fronts have finger holes in them).

Step 2
Mark a cross in the center of the back of each drawer and drill a hole to fit the screw size of the drawer handles.

Step 3
Gently sand down the whole unit and the drawers, making sure you work in the direction of the grain of the wood. Wipe each piece with a slightly damp cloth to remove any wood dust.

2

3

Step 4

Take the paint in the color that you want to paint the body of the unit and pour a little of it into a plastic cup. Then add water to dilute the paint—approximately 8 parts water to 1 part paint. Since the unit will be color washed it is not necessary to prime it first. Apply the diluted paint using light, fluid movements and painting in the direction of the wood grain (see *Color washing* below).

Step 5

Dilute all the other paints that you are going to use—8 parts water to 1 part paint—and then color wash all the drawers.

Step 6

Color wash the four wooden handles for the feet in the same colors as the drawer fronts.

4

5

6

Color washing

Color washing is one of the simplest and most effective ways of painting wood. It picks up and highlights the grain of the wood beautifully, and thus it is not necessary to prime the wood first. Since the paint is diluted with water it is vital that you start off with a water-based latex—the finished effect is slightly translucent.

Apply the watered-down paint mixture with light strokes of the paintbrush, working in the same direction as the grain of the wood. You will need to work fast because this solution will be absorbed into the wood. Because only small quantities of paint are used, buy the smallest cans available.

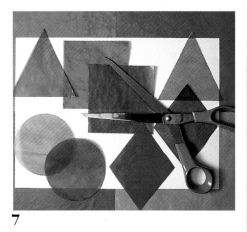

7

Step 7

Cut out two each of circles, squares, triangles, and diamonds from the colored tissue paper to a size that will fit comfortably on the front of each drawer.

Step 8

Using the spray glue, lightly spray each paper shape and then paste one shape onto the front of each drawer.

Step 9

Use wood glue to attach the wooden feet to the bottom of the unit. When they have just begun to set, varnish the bottom of the unit and allow it to dry overnight.

8

9

Day Two

Step 10
Varnish the whole unit and drawers with clear matte varnish. Ideally, you should apply three to four coats, letting each coat dry for approximately four hours in between.

Step 11
When the varnish is completely dry, screw the handles on the front of each drawer.

Varnishing

Varnishing an item of furniture helps to protect it against wear and tear. It also gives you the option of changing the surface from an eggshell finish to matte to gloss. Durable, hard varnishes are slightly yellow in color, while colorless varnishes offer less protection.
I recommend that you select a matte finish for your varnish, as it does not catch the light and bring out all the irregularities on the furniture.

10

11

Playing card curtains and tiebacks

Make bedtime more fun for children with these playing card shapes. I have chosen bright primary blue to go with red instead of the traditional black.

Planning your time

DAY ONE
AM: Cut out the shapes
PM: Make all the padded shapes

DAY TWO
AM: Cut out tabs and attach to the curtains, then sew on shapes
PM: Make the tiebacks

Tools and materials

Fabric for the tab tops, shapes, and tiebacks

2oz (55g) batting

Fabric for the curtains and lining (twice the width of the window)

Scissors

Thick brown paper for cutting templates

The approach to decorating windows has changed dramatically since the 1980s. Now there are many more options to choose from than just a plain curtain rod. Curtain poles are extremely popular and look particularly good in children's bedrooms. Avoid the sophisticated wrought-iron poles and instead opt for wooden ones that are more adaptable to decoration. If you buy them in their natural wood state they are very easy to paint in a bright color.

The tab tops on these curtains are also easy to make, though the padded shapes may take a little time to master. Once you have perfected making these shapes, however, you will have no difficulty with any of the other projects in the book that use a similar technique.

Tab top curtains save on curtain tape and hooks—the tabs are simply fed onto the wooden pole. This type of heading does make it a little difficult for the curtains to be pulled back as far as you may wish, however, so I have designed matching tiebacks to hold back the bulk of the curtains during the day.

Day One

Step 1

Trace the playing card templates on page 73 onto brown paper and cut them out. Enlarge two of them for the tiebacks.

Step 2

Measure the width of the curtain and calculate how many tabs and shapes you will need. I have placed mine 6" (15cm) apart. Then, using your templates, cut out as many pairs of shapes as you need. Also cut one piece of batting for each shape.

Step 3

Place each pair of shapes right sides together on top of the batting. Machine sew all the way around the shape. Make a cut in the middle of each shape through one of the pieces of fabric and pull the whole shape through. Repeat this for all the shapes, including the two large ones.

Day Two

Step 4

Cut out the required number of tabs, each measuring 8x16" (20x40cm). Fold the tabs in half lengthwise, with right sides together, and machine sew around the two sides leaving a short top edge open. Turn right side out and press with an iron.

Step 5

Separately hem the curtain fabric and lining (at the bottom), but do not sew them together. Lay the curtain and lining right sides together, then fold the tabs in half and pin them on along the top edge, leaving 6" (15cm) between each. The folded length of the tabs should be between the two pieces of fabric. Now machine stitch a straight line all the way across the top edge of the curtain to secure the tabs in place.

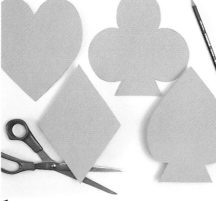

1

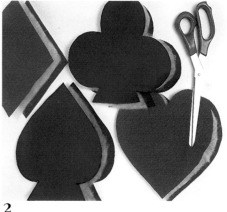

2

3

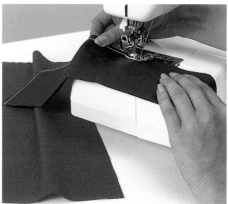

4

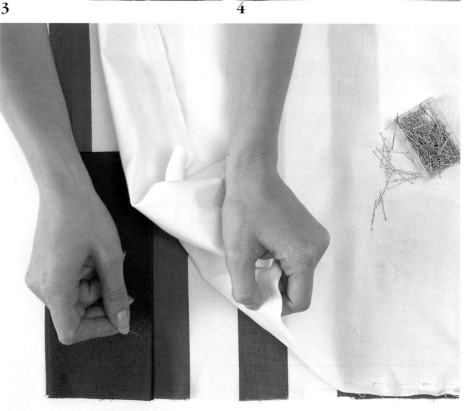

5

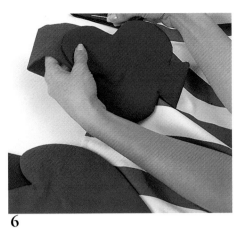

6

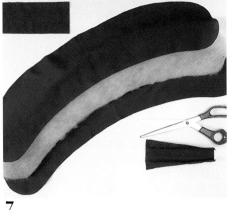

7

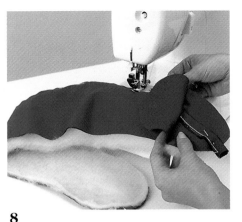

8

Step 6

With the right sides of the curtains still together, machine sew down the side edges of the curtains to secure lining and curtain fabric together. Then turn the curtains right side out and hand sew a shape onto each tab.

Step 7

Cut out the tieback pieces. These are crescent shapes 6x28" (15x70cm) with rounded ends. For each tieback you will need two pieces of crescent-shaped fabric and one piece of batting. You will also need two tabs 3x7" (8x18cm), one for each end. Take the tabs and fold both long edges into the center, fold together again into the center and press with an iron. Then machine sew a line down the centers to secure them in their folded-up state.

Step 8

Take the crescent-shaped pairs and sandwich them, right sides together, with the batting underneath. Insert the tabs, one at each end, folded in half lengthwise between the fabric, and machine stitch all the way around, securing the tabs in place. Leave a small opening along one side and turn the tieback right side out and hand sew it closed.

Step 9

Take the extra-large padded shapes and hand sew them onto one end of the tieback—not the middle!

9

Machine sewing and turning right side out

Many of the projects in the book include making shaped fabric pieces that need to be machine sewn on the wrong sides and turned right side out. Corners need to be clipped—to do this, cut across the seam allowance after sewing the seam, but leave at least ¼" (6mm) between the seam and the cut edge of the fabric. Likewise, on fabric shapes make little snips into the seam allowance, but be careful not to get too close to the seam. This will prevent pulling once it is turned right side out.

Elephant pocket storage system

This reliable elephant carries lots of jewel-bright pockets of different shapes and sizes to help your children keep track of personal accessories and special treasures.

Children always seem to fill their pockets with the strangest assortment of what they regard as basic essentials. So I have taken this theme and turned it into a larger and more practical version. A friendly elephant forms the base upon which hangs an assortment of bright pockets decorated with a variety of colorful trinkets.

I have used batting for making the elephant base to give it more substance, and it also helps to accentuate the machine-sewn detailing of the feet, ear, and eye.

Make sure you choose a heavyweight fabric for the pocket system base since it will need to bear the strain of a great number of items jammed into the pockets. You can make as many pockets as you like, large and small, and of course, they do not have to form part of an animal. You could machine sew them onto a plain piece of fabric. Sew a channel across the top and bottom, and place wooden dowels into the channels to help the pocket system hang better.

Planning your time

DAY ONE
AM: Cut out all the pieces and machine sew the pockets together

PM: Machine sew body together and attach pockets

DAY TWO
AM: Embroider face and foot details and sew on decorations

Tools and materials

Heavyweight fabric for the pocket system base

Brightly colored fabrics for the pockets, preferably cotton twill

4oz (115g) batting for the elephant's body

Decorations, beads, and foil shapes, or fabric pens

Scissors

Chalk

Day One

Step 1

Using the chalk, draw the elephant shape onto the fabric, following the templates on page 74. Cut out two elephant shapes in fabric, and cut one in batting.

Step 2

Following the shape of the elephant's back, cut out two purple "blankets" from the cotton twill—the pockets will later be attached to this blanket.

Step 3

Using different colored cotton twill fabrics, cut out four different shaped pockets that will neatly fit onto the purple blanket—you will need two of each pocket shape.

Step 4

Place the right sides of the purple blanket together and machine sew around the three edges, leaving the top curved edge open. Turn it right side out and press with a warm iron.

Step 5

Place each pair of pockets right sides together. Sew around all the edges, leaving a small opening on one side. Turn them all right side out and press with a warm iron. Then hand sew the opening (see page 25).

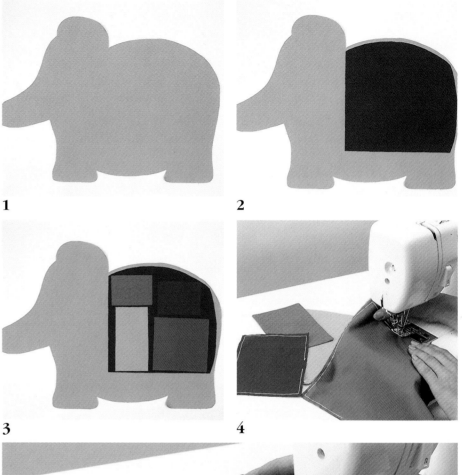

2

5

Planning the pockets

Bear in mind the height of your children when making the pocket system. They must be able to reach into the pockets with ease. In general, the younger the child, the wider and shallower the pockets should be.

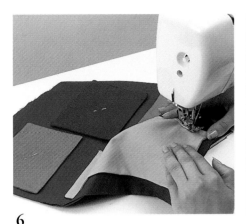

6

7

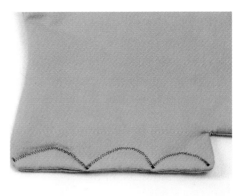

8

Step 6

Pin the pockets in position on the purple blanket and machine sew around three sides of each pocket, leaving the top edge open. Repeat this row of stitches for extra strength.

Step 7

Place the elephant body pieces right sides together, but sandwich the now-completed purple blanket in between them with the curved tops lined up. Place the batting at the back of this "sandwich" and machine sew all the way around the elephant, leaving the side seam open at the rear of the elephant. Repeat this row of stitches for extra strength. Pull the whole elephant through the open seam to turn it right side out and then hand sew the rear seam.

Day Two

Step 8

Using a zigzag stitch, machine sew the feet, ear, and eye details with a contrasting color thread.

Step 9

Sew the decorations onto the front of the pockets and over the eye. Sew two fabric loops onto the back of the elephant so that it can be attached to the wall. Finally, sew a shoelace or other type of cord onto the elephant for a tail.

9

Decorating the pockets

Besides sewing on beads and foils you could also decorate the pockets with fabric pens. They come in a variety of bright colors and textures. Also look for glitter pens that dispense glitter in a glue solution.

Porthole blackboard

Small children may draw to their hearts' content on this blackboard in the shape of a porthole. The fishy erasers and pockets continue the seafaring theme.

Normally, parents try to keep their children's artistic endeavors off the walls, but here I have created a wall chalkboard, which children can happily attack with as many colors of chalk as they wish. Blackboard paint is available in quart cans and is applied straight onto a plain painted wall. There is nothing to stop you from painting a whole wall with this paint and the beauty of it is that you can paint over it with ordinary paint at any time. A thick cloth is all it takes to remove any budding Picasso's works of art.

The cloth and chalk are all neatly kept together on a little hanging rod. Blue terry cloth pockets are perfect for keeping the chalk in and are decorated with a bright orange fish. The terry cloth starfish eraser hangs from a hook and can easily be washed out when it becomes too chalky. The theme for this project was the sea, hence the fun porthole-shaped chalkboard, starfish, and fish accessories, but you could change the shapes to suit your own children's favorite themes.

Planning your time

DAY ONE

AM: Cut template, spray frame, and paint blackboard

PM: Make clay "rivets" and starfish; screw hooks into wall

DAY TWO

AM: Make terry cloth pockets and orange fish

PM: Make the starfish eraser and assemble the rod

Tools and materials

Thick brown paper for porthole template

Silver spray paint

Blackboard paint

Paintbrush

Yellow polymer clay

Three plastic-coated screw-in hooks, plastic anchors, and drill

⅝" (1.5cm) wooden dowel cut to the width of the porthole— 37" (92cm)

Orange oil-based paint

All-purpose glue

Blue and yellow terry cloth

Orange cotton twill

2oz (55g) batting for the fish shapes

24" (60cm) of orange satin ribbon, ⅜" (1cm) wide

5" (12cm) of blue satin ribbon, ⅜" (1cm) wide

Black fabric pen

Scissors

Artist's spray glue

Day One

Step 1

Draw the design for the frame of the porthole onto brown paper (see page 75). Here the porthole frame is 3½" (9cm) deep around a center circle of 29" (72cm) in diameter. Remember to leave some brown paper all the way around the outer edge of the porthole frame. After cutting out the frame, apply some spray glue to the reverse sides of the template and then position it on the wall at the desired height. Place the central cutout circle in the middle. Make sure that all the edges are firmly stuck to the wall, then give the frame a light application of silver spray paint. Remove the templates from the wall.

Step 2

Carefully paint in the center of the porthole with the blackboard paint, paying particular attention to the edges.

Step 3

Roll and cut out eight 1½" (4cm) circles, each ⅝" (1.5cm) thick, out of the polymer clay. Using a sharp implement, score each with a "rivet" down the center. Bake following the manufacturer's instructions. When they are cool, place them on a piece of newspaper and lightly spray paint them silver. Mark around the porthole eight evenly spaced crosses, and stick the silver rivets onto them using the all-purpose glue. Mark under the porthole the positions for the three hooks, drill the holes, insert a plastic anchor into each one, and then screw in the hooks.

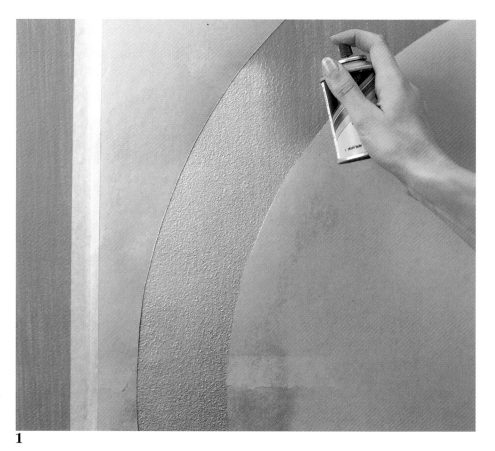

1

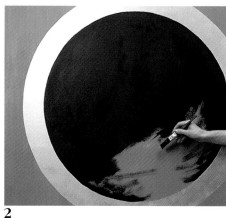

2

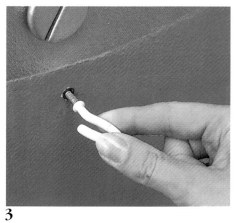

3

Drawing a circle

In order to draw a very large circle onto your template, use a pushpin to attach a piece of string to the paper. Measure out the radius of your required circle and cut the string to this length, adding enough to tie a pencil on the end. Then, holding your finger over the pushpin, take the pencil and rotate it through 360° to draw the circle. Repeat this process, shortening the string by 3½" (9cm), to draw the inner edge of the porthole frame.

Step 4

Apply primer to the wooden dowel and allow to dry. Then paint the dowel with the orange paint and allow to dry. Using the yellow polymer clay, make two flat starfish shapes. Bake them following the manufacturer's instructions, and when cool, glue them to each end of the wooden dowel.

Day Two

Step 5

Cut out the blue terry cloth pockets with the selvage edge running across the top of them. You will need four pieces, each measuring 9" (22cm) wide and 10" (25cm) deep. Place them in pairs, right sides together, and machine sew the three sides. Then turn them right side out.

Step 6

Cut the orange ribbon into four lengths of 6" (15cm) and hand sew two ribbon loops onto the back piece of each pocket.

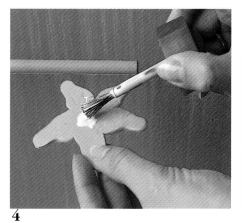
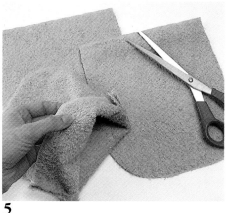

4

5

Using sprays

When using spray paint and spray glue make sure that the room you are working in is well ventilated. Protect any surfaces near the area that you are spraying— spray paint, especially, has a tendency to go everywhere.

6

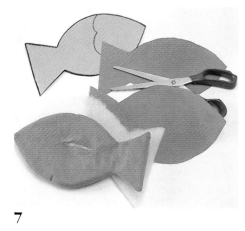

7

8

Step 7

Using the outlines on page 75, make a template for the fish out of brown paper. Use it to cut out four fish shapes from the orange fabric and two from the batting. Place the fish in pairs, right sides together, and put the batting at the back of the fabric. Machine sew all the way around. Then make a small slit through the center of one piece of the orange fabric and turn the fish right side out. Press with a warm iron.

Step 8

Use a black fabric pen to draw eyes and gills onto the fabric fish and then hand sew the fish onto the fronts of the blue pockets.

Step 9

Cut out a template for the starfish and use it to cut out two starfish shapes from the yellow terry cloth fabric. Place them right sides together and machine sew the starfish all the way around, leaving an opening on one leg. Turn it through the opening right side out and then hand sew it closed. Hand sew the blue ribbon onto the end of a leg to form a loop.

9

10

Step 10

Feed both the pockets onto the dowel through their loops and position in place on the hooks. Attach the starfish; simply hang it on the middle hook by its loop.

Step 11

To complete the marine theme I added some pre-cut particle board trim to the baseboard. Cut into a wave shape and painted, it blends in with the baseboard while still providing a fun element to the whole room scheme.

Using particle board trim

Pre-cut particle board trim is an easy way of adding instant interest to straight edges. Painted to blend in or contrast with whatever you put it with, it provides a finishing touch that helps to complete the decoration of a room.

11

Painted and stamped toy chest

Toy chests provide useful storage for a host of toys and games. This one rests on elegant feet—in contrast to the friendly informality of its contents.

A chest or blanket box is an invaluable item of furniture in a child's bedroom because it is perfect for storing big, bulky toys and games, while also doubling as a low table or a seat. Wooden chests come in all sizes. Some are plain, while others, like the one I transformed in this project, have a little detailing cut into the front panel and, more importantly, have feet. I always feel that a piece of furniture with feet on it immediately takes on a more stylish look—raising this chest off the ground helps to give definition to its shape.

This toy chest came flat packed and ready to assemble. I painted it with four bright pastel colors, then used a rubber stamp to apply the yellow block design and hand painted some wavy lines. The finishing touch was the addition of two chunky rope handles.

Since I wanted the box to have a chalky look to it I used water-based latex paints. But to make sure that it would survive any child's rough handling it was given a couple of coats of matte varnish. If you prefer, however, you could paint it with more durable gloss paint, although bear in mind that you will end up with a shiny effect.

Planning your time

DAY ONE
AM: Drill, sand, and prime chest

PM: Paint the chest

DAY TWO
AM: Assemble chest, apply stamp design and wavy line, and varnish

PM: Varnish two more times and tie on rope

Tools and materials

One flat-packed ready-to-assemble toy chest

Screwdriver

Drill and large drill bit

Masking tape

Fine-grit sandpaper

All-in-one white primer and undercoat

Selection of complementary latex paints

Paintbrushes, including a small artist's brush

Clear matte varnish

60" (1.5m) each of two colors of rope

Stamp design

Mini roller

Dish for paint

1

2

3

Day One

Step 1
Using masking tape, mark where the four holes for the rope handles will be on the lid of the chest. I positioned them 6" (15cm) from the edge, with 8" (20cm) between the two holes of each handle. Use a large drill bit and drill the four holes through the lid.

Step 2
Gently sand all the surfaces of the chest on both sides to provide a key, or rough surface, for the primer. Wipe down with a damp cloth to remove all the wood dust.

Step 3
Apply a coat of an all-in-one quick primer and undercoat, and then allow to dry.

Step 4
Decide which sides of the chest to paint in which color, then paint them using latex paint. Paint the pieces on both sides, allowing to dry. Also paint the feet.

4

Buying a toy chest
If you are going to buy a new toy or blanket chest to transform, look for ones that are untreated—that is, not painted or varnished. This will save you time, since any layers of paint and varnish must be removed before you can apply the decoration described here.

Day Two

Step 5
Assemble the chest following the manufacturer's instructions.

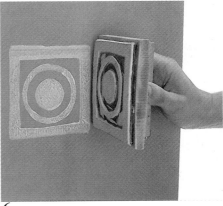

Step 6
Mark lightly with a pencil where you want to apply the stamp design. I placed designs over each of the drilled holes on the lid, two on the front and back, and one on each side. Pour a little paint of the color chosen for the design into a small dish, then roll the mini roller in the paint so that it is evenly covered. Roll the paint onto the stamp and gently apply the stamp to the chest.

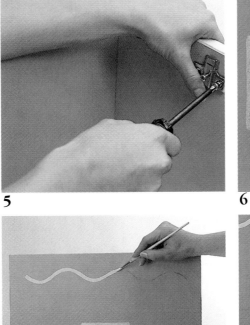

Step 7
Using a pencil, lightly draw the wavy lines on each side of the toy chest. When you are happy with them, use the fine paintbrush to paint over the lines. As an extra touch I painted dots along the wavy line in a contrasting color. Allow to dry.

Step 8
Using a clear matte varnish, apply two to three coats all over the chest inside and out, making sure that each coat dries thoroughly in between.

Step 9
Thread the colored rope through the holes and tie large, chunky knots on the underside of the lid. Remember to leave enough slack to form adequate handles on the top of the chest.

Paints for stamping
You can buy special paints for stamping but I found that using a water-based latex paint worked just as well on the toy chest.

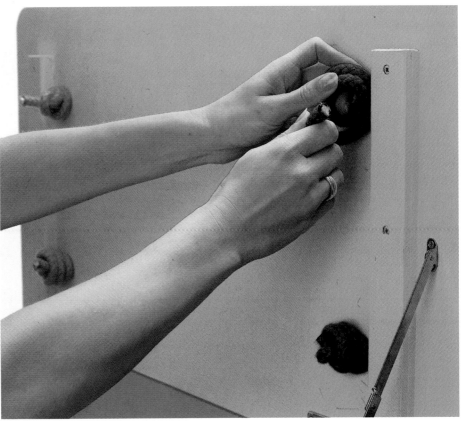

Templates

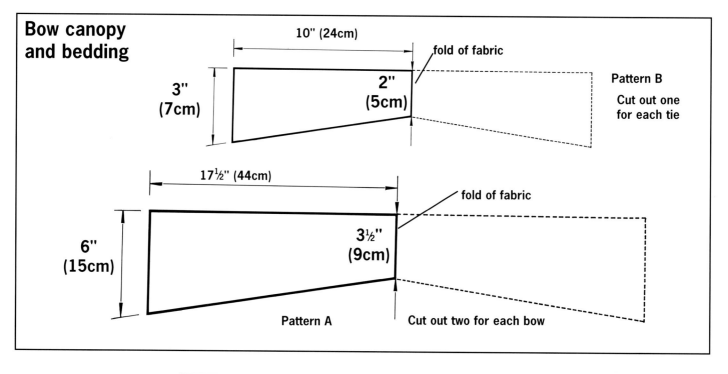

Bow canopy and bedding

10" (24cm)

3" (7cm)

2" (5cm)

fold of fabric

Pattern B

Cut out one for each tie

17½" (44cm)

6" (15cm)

3½" (9cm)

fold of fabric

Pattern A

Cut out two for each bow

"Daisy daisy" bulletin board

Tic-tac-toe headboard game

Templates

Fat-cat beanbag

47"
(118cm)

30" (75cm)

Templates

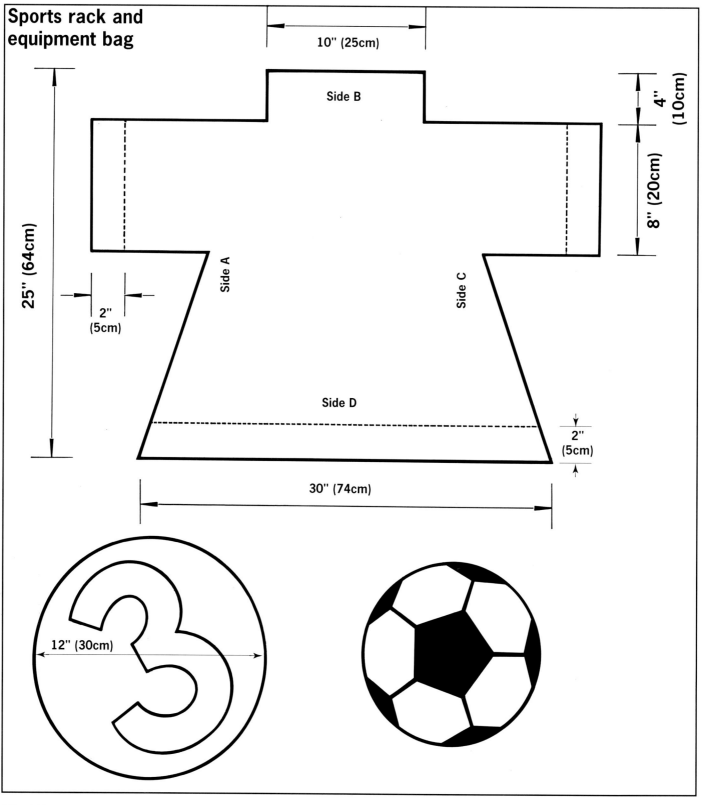

Sports rack and equipment bag

10" (25cm)

Side B

4" (10cm)

8" (20cm)

25" (64cm)

Side A

Side C

2" (5cm)

Side D

2" (5cm)

30" (74cm)

12" (30cm)

Templates

Playing card curtains and tiebacks

Templates

Elephant pocket storage system

Templates

Porthole blackboard

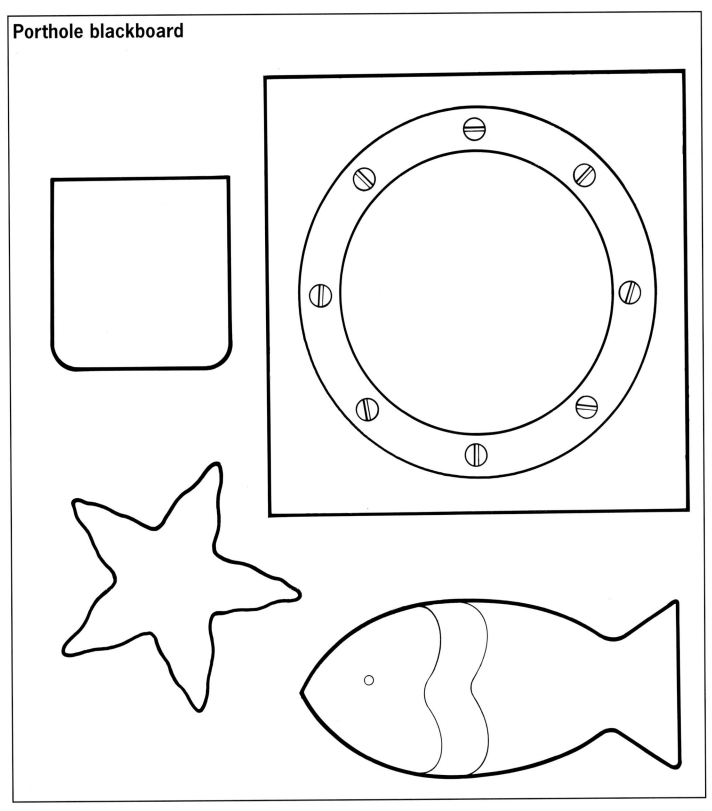

Glossary

Particle board

Paint rollers

Masking tape

Drill bits

Awl
A pointed tool used for marking the position for drilling a hole.

Batting
Fabric stuffing available in different thicknesses (weights). The type used in this book is polyester and fully washable once inside its fabric cover.

Color washing
A paint technique using watered-down latex paint to produce a chalky finish.

Dowel
A length of round wood with a small diameter that can easily be to cut to whatever length required.

Drill/drill bits
When buying a power drill make sure that the motor is powerful enough for all tasks; some drills with very low speed settings can be used for putting in screws. Bits are available in various sizes for drilling different-sized holes.

French seam
A strong seam that does not show any additional stitching line from the right side of

the fabric. It can be used only on straight edges.

Glaze
Not to be confused with varnish. A glaze is a transparent medium to which color is added in the form of universal stainers (tinting colors).

Glue (all-purpose)
Can be used to stick a variety of materials together.

Glue (artist's spray glue)
Provides a light coating of glue out of a spray can.

Glue (wood)
Specifically for sticking items to wood.

Heavy brown paper
You can use brown paper, tracing paper, or graph paper for making a pattern or template.

Key
A rough surface suitable for the adhesion of paint or glue, usually achieved by rubbing the surface with sandpaper.

Masking tape
Adhesive tape that has multiple decorating uses

and is ideal for masking areas when painting. Available in different widths.

Paint (blackboard)
A special paint available from hardware stores that is painted onto wooden surfaces or plain walls to produce a wipeable surface that can be drawn on with chalk.

Paint (latex)
A water-based paint that is easy to use and can be applied with a paintbrush or roller. It provides a water-resistant coating and is available in both matte and satin finishes. It is fast drying, so you need to work quickly with it.

Paint (oil-based)
This is available in gloss, eggshell, and matte finishes and produces a durable and waterproof coating. It should be applied in layers, beginning with a primer and undercoat. Oil-based paints take longer to dry; large items should be left overnight to dry completely.

Paintbrushes
Select an appropriate size brush according to the size

of the item you are painting. Artist's brushes are useful for painting for intricate details.

Paint rollers
These are ideal when you are painting large surface areas. Look for patterned foam rollers that create an interesting texture on a flat surface.

Particle board
Strong board made from soft wood fibers bonded together under pressure. It is sanded to produce an extremely smooth surface.

Plastic wall anchor
Use a plastic anchor that matches the screw size when making wall attachments.

Polymer clay
Available in a variety of fun colors, it must be baked according to the manufacturer's instructions to produce a hard, durable finish.

Priming
New or stripped wood should be given a coat of primer before anything else is applied to it. This provides a good base for the top coat

and therefore a more professional-looking overall finish. Look for primers and undercoats that are combined (all-in-one) since they will save valuable time. Previously painted wood does not need a primer, but sand down old paint to provide a good key for the undercoat.

Sanding block
Sandpaper wrapped around a wood block to make the job of sanding easier.

Selvage
The edges of fabric that run down both sides of a length of fabric. These edges are finished and do not fray.

Slipstitch
Used where a seam is required along the right side of a fabric.

Spackle
Ideal for filling holes, you can buy this in packets and then add to water to make a paste or buy ready-to-use spackle in a tub.

Stainproofing treatment
A finish that can be applied to fabric that gives it a stain-resistant surface.

Stamping
Making and applying inked designs to a smooth surface.

Staple gun
Larger than a domestic stapler, a staple gun is very powerful and can be used to secure fabric on wood.

Tacks
Small, thin nails.

Varnish (oil-based)
This is the most traditional varnish, but is also the slowest drying, taking 12 to 24 hours.

Varnish (polyurethane)
Available in matte, semigloss, and gloss finishes, it dries within four hours and gives a very durable surface.

Varnishing
Used for sealing a wooden surface and making it more durable. Most painted surfaces look better when treated with varnish.

Velcro
Brand name for a hook and loop fastener that consists of two pieces of nylon, one with tiny hooks and the other with loops, that adhere when pressed together.

Stamp and small roller

Oil-based paints

Sanding block

Polymer clay

Suppliers

GENERAL CRAFT

Hobby Lobby
7707 SW 44th Street
Oklahoma City, OK 73179
Tel: (405) 745-1100
www.hobbylobby.com

Michaels Arts & Crafts
8000 Bent Branch Drive
Irving, TX 75063
Tel: (214) 409-1300
www.michaels.com

Zim's Crafts, Inc.
4370 South 300 West
Salt Lake City, UT 84107
Toll free: (800) 453-6420
Tel: (801) 268-2505
Fax: (801) 268-9859
www.zimscrafts.com

GENERAL ART SUPPLIES

Jo-Ann Fabrics and Crafts
www.joann.com
(website includes store locator)
Store questions: (888) 739-4120

HARDWARE/ HOME IMPROVEMENT STORES

Home Depot U.S.A., Inc.
2455 Paces Ferry Road
Atlanta, GA 30339-4024
Tel: (770) 433-8211
www.homedepot.com

Lowe's Home Improvement Warehouse
Customer Care (ICS7)

Lowe's Companies, Inc.
P.O. Box 1111
North Wilkesboro, NC 28656
Toll free: (800) 44-LOWES
www.lowes.com

PAINT PRODUCTS

Delta Technical Coatings
2550 Pellissier Place
Whittier, CA 90601
Toll free: (800) 423-4135
Fax: (562) 695-5157
www.deltacrafts.com
Acrylic, glass, and fabric paints.

EK Success
P.O. Box 1141
Clifton, NJ 07014-1141
Toll free: (800) 524-1349
success@eksuccess.com
www.eksuccess.com
Paints and general craft products.

Pébéo of America
P.O. Box 714
Route 78, Airport Rd.
Swanton, VT 05488
Toll free: (800) 363-5012
Fax: (819) 821-4151
Glass paints, markers, and mediums.

Liquitex-Binney and Smith
P.O. Box 431
Easton, PA 18044-0431
Tel: (888) 422-7954
www.liquitex.com
Paints, mediums, varnishes, and additives.

PAINTBRUSHES

Loew-Cornell
563 Chestnut Ave.
Teaneck, NJ 07666-2490
Tel: (201) 836-7070
Fax: (201) 836-8110
www.loew-cornell.com

FABRIC CRAFTS/NOTIONS

Coats & Clark
P.O. Box 27067
Greenville, NC 29616
Toll free: (800) 648-1479
www.coatsandclark.com
General purpose threads.

Dharma Trading Co.
P.O. Box 150916
San Rafael, CA 94915
Toll free: (800) 542-5227
catalog@dharmatrading.com
www.dharmatrading.com
Fabric dyes, paints, and fabric art products.

STENCILS

American Traditional Stencils
442 First New Hampshire Turnpike
Northwood, NH 03261-3401
Tel: (603) 942-8100
www.americantraditional.com

Royal Design Studio
2504 Transportation Ave., Suite H
National City, CA 91950
Toll free: (800) 747-9767
www.royaldesignstudio.com

Index